Praise for The Ya

"In my top 10 all time favorite bc
Amazon reviewer: 5 stars. This bc
and taught me what I was seeking ... This book breaks down yogic teachings into easily digestible bites, allowing us to gather what we need and come back for more when we are ready. This is a book we should all return to year after year so we can be reminded how to live with a right spirit and be good humans.

"The Foundation of Yoga!" Chrisy R., Amazon reviewer: 5 stars. This book is the perfect addition to my practice of Yoga. This book is beautifully written and easy to comprehend. After reading the first chapter, I was so inspired that I ordered five more copies to donate to my local yoga studio for students to borrow.

"Excellent book, easy to understand." Drew H., Amazon reviewer: 5 stars. This is a fantastic book for anyone, yogi or not. I'm not a non fiction reader, but I'm instantly drawn in by the writing style. It's as if Deborah Adele is drawing my awareness to truths I already knew, but didn't know I knew.

"Read this book!" Gail C., Amazon reviewer: 5 stars. I have loved this book for years; it creates a beautiful space for personal development and learning how we can move through life with more peace and ease. It's a good read for yogis and non yogis; there are benefits for everyone in this book. Thank you to the author for this lovely gift.

Praise for The Kleshas

"Clear, deep and practical." Gina C., Amazon reviewer: 5 stars. I've read many books that include sections on the kleshas and they're good. This book is GREAT. Deborah's writing style is clear, concise and practically oriented (vs too mystical to comprehend) without sacrificing the potency and depth of these teachings. Can't say enough about this book, for me the kleshas are IT - the greatest gift of the sutras. She really does them justice!

"Distills ancient wisdom." Beth G., Advance Review
It takes a special talent to distill knowledge from an ancient wisdom tradition into a practical guide for a contemporary audience. In *The Kleshas*, Deborah Adele has condensed years of practice, learning and teaching into this down-to-earth, informative, and inspirational book. The personal experiences and the reflections she offers will encourage you to take the lessons off the page and into your everyday life.
~Beth Gibbs, author of *Enlighten Up! Finding Clarity, Contentment and Resilience in a Complicated World*,
www.bethgibbs.com

"A remarkable, practical manual for learning to manage our mind and behaviors." Sarah H., Advance Review. Born from the heart of yoga, it offers the modern reader a practical approach for healing our own inner conflicts, and the divisiveness that is tearing at the deep fabric of society. Timeless wisdom presented in relatable, actionable steps that anyone can follow. ~ Sarah Hutchinson R.N., E-RYT 500, Ayurvedic Yoga Educator, www.yogabeyondtheposes.com

The Yamas & Niyamas Embodied

THE YAMAS & NIYAMAS EMBODIED: a companion journal

Published by:
Votre Vie LLC / Duluth, Minnesota 55812
Votre Vie LLC is a subsidiary of On-Word Bound Books, LLC.

Fonts used:
Main text: Adobe Garamond Pro.
Titles and quotes: Shangri La and Rowen Oak by Nick's Fonts
http://www.nicksfonts.com/

Sanskrit was illustrated by Sara Duke and approved by Vyaas Houston of the American Sanskrit Institute.

Printed on Demand

10 9 8 7 6 5 4 3 2 1

The Yamas & Niyamas Embodied

a companion journal

by Deborah Adele

Votre Vie, LLC
Little French Press ~ Duluth, Minnesota

To this body...

that I love, hate,
care for, abuse,
enjoy, blame,
adorn, coddle,
push, delight in
and ignore.

Thank you for the gift
of embodiment.

Thank you for your endless
faithfulness and grace.

Table of Contents

Introduction

For over a decade now, I have been diligent in my practice of the yamas and niyamas. I have attempted to continue to unpack their deeper, more subtle meaning and to invite them into the decisions and challenges of my daily life. I have paid close attention to my interactions with others and to the beauty that arises when these principles are followed and the hurt and disturbance that arises when they are not. Most of all I am aware of their power and my need to practice them.

This book is the result of an eye-opening experience that changed my continued conversation with the yamas and niyamas. I hadn't realized it until that moment, but my own body had something to teach me, and I was finally willing to listen.

I remember the day it happened. It was an odd experience, for sure. I had been diligent in my practice of nonviolence when I found myself the recipient of an angry, rude taxi driver who, upon delivering me to my destination, threw my luggage including my computer bag harshly onto the pavement in the middle of the street. Instantaneously I felt rage flood my body and the uncontrollable need to avenge myself. But my body did something else. It took the rage and transformed it into kindness. I found myself uttering a sincere whisper of blessing to this man as I handed him a generous tip. In a moment of unexplainable timeless time, grace seemed to find a way in.

Even as I share this with you, it seems outlandish. Yet, there was no denial or suppression; nor was there any lingering residue. There was no need to repeat the story of the "mean taxi driver" over and over to myself or anyone else to confirm my need to feel violated. The event was over when it was over; the blessing I wished upon the driver was sincere. Whatever my body did, it did exquisitely and completely.

To this day, I don't understand what happened, and it doesn't really matter. What matters is that I began to include my body as one of my prime teachers on the yamas and niyamas. The truth is, the body is constantly carrying a lot of information; we have access to more clarity than our minds often let on. This book is an invitation to dialogue with the body by exploring what your body has to say about each of these ethical practices.

Accessing the Body's Voice (How to Use this Book)

With each yama and niyama, you will find a brief meditation along with a suggested posture. Read the meditation (or listen on YouTube*) and then come into the suggested pose in whatever ability your body allows.

If you are new to yoga or have limited physical ability, you may adapt the pose by staying seated or making other modifications. You could also do an internet search with the name of the pose plus the word "modified" or "with a chair" for ideas to form the shape with your body.

The difficulty of the pose is not important; it is the ease of your body and your mind's quality of attention that allows learning to happen. From this place of awareness and willingness to listen, be available to hear the body's wisdom.

You may find your body shifting into creative movement. Or if you are familiar with these poses, you may move through a vinyasa flow that incorporates all the yamas and niyamas. Either way, it becomes a beautiful, moving meditation, grounding your body, your mind, and your day in these principles of right relationship.

Remember, this is not about "doing" a pose, nor is it about the mechanics of a pose. It is about using the pose to learn about embodied ethics.

Take time after each body exploration to reflect, journal, or sit in silence before moving on. Take time to discover what your body has to teach you about each yama and niyama. Can you feel the essence of each guideline in every cell of your being?

Following the body meditation, you will find additional questions which invite you to keep your awareness inward, listening to and learning from the innate wisdom of the body. Answer these questions as if your body was answering, not your head. The answer may or may not surprise you. Be willing to be surprised. In addition, you may choose to draw pictures or use colored pencils or use your non-dominant hand to access your inner knowing.

You can choose to do one yama or niyama daily, weekly, or stay with one guideline for a whole month before moving on to the next one. If a challenge has presented itself in your life, you may want to stay engaged with the yama or niyama that speaks to that challenge. Whatever the challenge, grounding your whole self in the body will offer support, clarity and reassurance.

* Scan this QR code with your camera app to join Deborah on YouTube for guided meditation on each yama and niyama. (Led and narrated by Deborah Adele.)

What are the Yamas & Niyamas?

Human life is a mixed experience. While seeking to feel good, we often feel empty; while seeking to feel fulfilled, we often feel our life has no purpose; while seeking to make a difference, we often feel no clear direction of action.

Yoga philosophy names the reason for this mixed human experience wrought with sadness and disappointment: the kleshas. (See *The Kleshas: Exploring the Elusiveness of Happiness* by Deborah Adele.) Yoga philosophy also suggests a way to shift our lives from this oscillating pattern into one of balance and fulfillment. The path leading from fluctuation and uncertainty to one of stability and contentment is called Ashtanga Yoga, or the 8-limbed path, and it begins with the yamas and niyamas.

We are not told why the yamas and niyamas hold such a place of importance, but we can surmise their significance for doing relationships well. And really, isn't everything a relationship? We have a relationship with those we know and those we don't know, with the climate and politics, with religion and the Higher Reality, with our practice, our work, and with ourselves. Learning to do all our relationships well is called ethical living. Growing ourselves in authenticity and integrity in all our relationships is imperative for creating a climate we and others can thrive in. The practice of the yamas & niyamas sets us on this trajectory.

Yoga is a sophisticated system that extends far beyond doing yoga postures; it is literally a way of living. Yoga is designed to bring you more and more awareness of not only your body but also your thoughts. The teachings are a practical, step-by-step methodology that bring understanding to your experiences, while at the same time pointing the way to the next experience. They are like a detailed map, telling you where you are and how to look for the next landmark. They facilitate taking ownership of your life and directing it towards the fulfillment that you seek.

The first limb of the 8-limbed path is comprised of five yamas, a Sanskrit word which translates literally into the word "restraints" and includes nonviolence, truthfulness, nonstealing, nonexcess, and nonpossessiveness. The second limb of the 8-limbed path is comprised of five niyamas, or "observances," and includes purity, contentment, self-discipline, self-study, and surrender.

Many guides to ethical conduct may leave us feeling overwhelmed with concepts or boxed in by rule sets. Yoga's guidelines do not limit us from living life, but rather they begin to open life up to us more and more fully, and they flow easily into one another in ways that are practical and easy to grasp.

Nonviolence (Ahimsa) is foundational to all the guidelines that follow, which in turn enhance the meaning and flesh out the richness of nonviolence. At the core of nonviolence is the essence of all yoga philosophy: First, do no harm. How do we live life to the fullest without causing harm to ourselves or another?

Truthfulness (Satya) is partnered with nonviolence. The marriage of these two guidelines is a powerful dance between two seeming opposites. We can appreciate this statement when we begin to practice speaking our truth without causing harm to others. As partners, truthfulness keeps nonviolence from being a wimpy cop-out, while nonviolence keeps truthfulness from being a brutal weapon. When they are dancing perfectly together, they create a spectacular sight. Their union is nothing short of profound love in its fullest expression. And when there is cause for disharmony or confusion between the two, truthfulness bows to nonviolence.

Nonstealing (Asteya) guides our right use of resources. What do we need to be happy? What do we need to fulfill our purpose on earth? What do we have that we don't need? What do we have that may be keeping others in lack? Often, our dissatisfaction with ourselves and our lives leads us to steal what is not rightfully ours. We steal from the earth, we steal from others, and we steal from ourselves. We steal from our own opportunity to grow ourselves into the person who has the right to have the life they want.

Nonexcess (Brahmacharya) literally means "walking with God." This guideline asks us to be aware of the sacredness of life and each moment that is lived. From this place of sacredness, we are primed to leave excess behind and live within the limits of enough. If we have been practicing nonstealing, we will automatically find ourselves prepared to practice this guideline.

Nonpossessiveness (Aparigraha) liberates us from emotional attachment. It reminds us that clinging to people and material objects only weighs us down and makes life a heavy and disappointing experience. When we practice letting go, we move ourselves toward freedom and an enjoyment of life that is expansive and fresh.

If we have begun to live the first five guidelines well, we may notice that our time is freeing up and there is more breathing space in our lives. The days begin to feel a little lighter and easier. Work is more enjoyable and our relationships with others are a little smoother. We like ourselves a little more; there is a lighter gait to our step; we realize that we need less than we previously thought; we are having more fun.

Following the yamas, we move into the subtle realm of the niyamas, toward an interior resting place, a place that becomes like Sabbath for us.

Purity (Saucha) is an invitation to cleanse our bodies, our attitudes, and our actions. It asks us to clean up our act so we can be more available to the qualities in life that we are seeking. This guideline also invites us to purify how we relate to what is uppermost in the moment. It is the quality of being aligned in our relationship with others, with the task at hand, and with ourselves.

Contentment (Santosha) cannot be sought. All the things we do to bring fulfillment to ourselves actually interfere with our own satisfaction and well-being. Contentment can only be found in acceptance and appreciation of what is in the moment. The more we learn to leave "what is" alone, the more contentment will quietly and steadily find us.

Self-Discipline (Tapas) literally means "heat" and can also be translated as catharsis or austerities. It is anything which provokes change. Change makes us spiritual heavyweights in the game of life; it is preparation for our own greatness. We all know how easy it is to be a person of high character when things are going our way, but what about those times life deals us a difficult hand? Who are we in those moments? This guideline invites us to purposefully seek refinement of our strength and character. Can we trust the heat? Can we trust the path of change itself?"

Self-Study (Svadhyaya) is the pursuit of knowing ourselves, studying what drives us and what shapes us because these things literally are the cause of the lives we are living. Self-study asks us to look at the stories we tell ourselves about ourselves and realize that these stories create the reality we are living. Ultimately, this guideline invites us to release the false and limiting self-perception our ego has imposed on us and know the truth of our Divine Self.

Surrender (Ishvara Pranidhana) reminds us that life knows what to do better than we do. Through devotion, trust, and active engagement, we can receive each moment with an open heart. Rather than paddling upstream, surrender is an invitation to go with the underlying current, enjoy the ride, and take in the view.

AHIMSA
Nonviolence

First, do no harm.

अहिंसा

Nonviolence

Nonviolence stands as the very core and foundation of all yoga philosophy and practice.

Peace. We long for it in our hearts, in our minds, and in our world. Yet violence is what we know. From stories on the news that we turn from in horror, to explosive words that find a way out of our mouth, violence is all too familiar.

Our bodies know violence well. When impatience, irritation, or anger arise in us, our muscles tense, our blood pressure rises, our breath freezes, and our sanity disappears. Unless we learn to read these early warnings from our body, we inevitably contribute to the disharmony in the world.

What are we to do? We can start by loving these bodies fiercely with good food, enough movement, kind thoughts, and sufficient rest and sleep. We can fine-tune our bodies so we can hear them warn us when we are about to be an untrustworthy member of the human race.

And then we can listen to our bodies. We can memorize what it feels like when we experience ease, contentment, and wellbeing. We can learn to feel the sense of kindness that overflows from us to others because we are so full of wellbeing ourselves, that kindness has nowhere else to go but outward to others.

Ahimsa: The Practice

We practice nonviolence in mountain pose, rooting our feet into the earth below us, and standing still like a mountain. We are simultaneously strong and relaxed, easy yet alert. We are learning to stand still when discontentment erupts around us or within us.

Bring yourself into mountain pose (standing or seated). When you feel established in this pose, bring your hands into prayer pose at the heart. Your hands are together with your thumbs gently pressing into your heart. Then, keeping your thumbs together at the heart, bend the large knuckles of your fingers outward, bringing your hands into *Kapota mudra* (Peace mudra / Dove mudra).

A mudra directs energy. Stand in this pose long enough to feel the energy of peace, love, and compassion circulating in your body. Memorize these sensations. At some point, you may find yourself wishing to share this feeling of peace, love, and compassion, sending these qualities out into the world with each exhalation.

Stay here as long as you wish. Take time to reflect, journal, or be in silence with this experience. Or you may choose to let your body move you into further exploration.

Intentionally choose your next activity. Whatever it is, do your best to maintain the feeling of nonviolence in your body and to consciously return to it throughout the day.

Kapota mudra (also known as Peace mudra or Dove mudra).

Scan the QR code below to join Deborah on YouTube for this guided practice.

The Body's Wisdom

We are learning to stand still when discontentment erupts around us or within us.

What can embodying mountain pose teach you about nonviolence?

What does your body have to say? You may choose to draw pictures, write with colored pencils, or use your non-dominant hand to access your inner knowing.

Courage

To create a life and a world free of violence is first and foremost to find our own courage.

I invite you to practice courage by doing one thing daily that you wouldn't normally do. What happens in your body before, during and after you do this one thing?

If you're feeling really brave, do one thing that scares you and get excited about the fact that you're scared and you're doing it anyway. See if you can discern between fear and the unfamiliar. Is there a different sensation in your body that accompanies this discernment?

Watch what happens to your sense of self and how your relationships with others might be different because you are courageously stepping into unknown territory. What happens?

Balance

Balance comes from listening to
the guidance and wisdom
of the inner voice.
When we are in balance,
we automatically live
in nonviolence.

Guard your balance as you would your most precious resource. Don't find your balance from a place in your head of what it should look like. Instead, find guidance from the messages of your body. In this moment, ask your body, "Do I need more sleep? More exercise? Do I need to eat differently? Do I need to pray? Do I need some variety in my life?"

Act on the messages of your body and explore what balance feels like. Note what you need and also note the effects on your life and on others.

Powerless

One of the biggest challenges to maintaining balance is feeling powerless. Nonviolence invites us to question the feeling of powerlessness, rather than accept it.

What are the sensations in your body when you feel powerless?

I often ponder the words of Yogiraj Achala, "I excite myself with my incompetencies." With this attitude, feelings of powerlessness become growth opportunities. What are some "growth opportunities" for you? What changes in your body when your thoughts change from powerlessness to opportunity?

Self-love

How we treat ourselves is in truth how we treat those around us.

For this whole week, pretend you are complete. There is no need to expect anything from yourself or to criticize or judge or change anything about yourself. No need to compete with anyone, no need to be more than you are (or less than you are). Note your experience.

Notice how much pleasure, kindness, and patience you can allow yourself to have with yourself. What do you notice? What happens in your body?

Also notice if being kind to yourself creates any discomfort or anxiety. Notice if there is a conflict between your beliefs and your body's voice.

Others

When we are unwilling to look deeply and courageously into our own lives, we can easily violate others in many subtle ways that we may not be aware of, thinking that we are actually helping them.

Watch where you are running interference on others' lives. Are you a worrier? A fixer? Discern the difference between "help" and "support." Do they feel different in your body?

Note the times you witnessed and supported without trying to change anything. How did this feel?

What might you be avoiding in your own life because you are so interested in others' lives?

Compassion

We learn compassion as
we dissolve our personal
version of the world,
and grow gentle eyes
that are not afraid to see
reality as it is.

Every human being walking this earth has painful stories tucked in the corners of their hearts. If we could remember this, perhaps we could see with the eyes of compassion rather than the eyes of our own judgments and preferences. What does judgment feel like in your body? What does compassion feel like in your body?

We learn compassion as we stop trying to change ourselves and others and choose instead to soften the boundaries that keep us separated from what we don't understand. We learn compassion as we do simple acts of kindness and allow others' lives to be as important as our own. What happens when you soften into what is and just let it be there?

We learn compassion as we stop living in our heads, where we can neatly arrange things, and ground ourselves in our bodies, where things might not be so neat. Press your feet to the floor and focus on your breath, deep in your belly, for 5 breaths, 5x a day. What do you notice?

SATYA
Truthfulness

The seeker of truth must be humble.

सत्य

Truthfulness

Satya or truthfulness, isn't safe, but it is good. Truth has the power to right wrongs and end sorrows. It is fierce in its demands and magnanimous in its offerings. It invites us to places we rarely frequent and where we seldom know what the outcome will be. Truth demands integrity to life and to our own self.

To practice truthfulness, we first need to know what truth is, and this is not an easy task. We often confuse truth with our beliefs, conditioning, perceptions, and opinions because they feel so real to us. In a cosmos more expansive than our minds can conceive, the "truth" we think we know is, at best, limited.

Throughout history the question, "What is truth?" has been asked, answered, and debated. The rise of the internet, social media, and the purposeful interference of trolling have increased the complexity of answers to that question. And in a growing world of polarization, we seem more intent on fighting for our perceived answers to this question rather than the diligent work of examining those answers.

Mahatma Gandhi, in his autobiography, explained that his whole life had been an experiment with truth. He gravitated towards something that felt right, experimented with it, learned from it, kept what he experienced as truthful and left the rest. In this way, he became a person respected by all. From his authenticity, the world was changed. What are we to learn from this? Humility. Gandhi said that whoever sought truth must be humbler than a speck of dust.

With so many truths floating around vying for our allegiance, often at dizzying speeds, there are things our bodies have to say. If we can loosen our defensive grip and relax our body, we are aware of the subtle sensation of alignment or misalignment within us. Our bodies seem to know if what we are hearing or reading feels congruent or noncongruent. But we must keep our bodies relaxed, our minds quiet, and our spirits humble to hear these subtle signals.

Satya: The Practice

Bring yourself into a position of humility. It could be a full prostration on the ground or a simple bowing of your head as you sit in a chair. Let your heart lead your head into the bow. Stay here long enough to let your body teach you about humility. What does it mean to be humbler than a speck of dust? Stay here as long as you wish. Take time to reflect, journal, or be in silence with this experience. Or you may let your body move you into further exploration.

When you feel complete, intentionally choose your next activity. Whatever it is, do your best to maintain the feelings of truthfulness and humility in your body and to consciously return to them throughout the day.

Scan the QR code on the right to join Deborah on YouTube for this guided practice.

The Body's Wisdom

We can become aware of the subtle sensation of alignment or misalignment within us.

What can embodying humility teach you about truthfulness?

What does your body have to say? You may choose to draw pictures, write with colored pencils, or use your non-dominant hand to access your inner knowing.

Be Real

My biggest fear is that everyone I know will be in the same room at the same time and I won't know who to be.

Observe the difference between "nice" and "real." Notice situations where you were nice. What did this experience invoke in you? How does your body feel when you are being nice?

Notice situations where you were real. What did this experience invoke in you? How does your body feel when you are being real?

From whom or what do you seek approval? Do you override your body's voice in favor of approval?

Self-Expression

Living the life
that cries to be lived
from the depth of our being
frees up our energy and vitality.

Spend some time in self-expression
(a day, a week, a month...)
What do you do to express yourself? In what way is your body part of your self-expression?

Make movement towards the external world with your internal hopes and dreams. Act on life-giving opportunities, despite the consequences. Observe what happens in your body. What do you notice?

If you find yourself in self-indulgence, ask yourself, "What does my body really want in this moment?"

Belong? Or Grow?

Human beings have both a need to belong to groups and a need to expand and grow.

What is happening in your body when you feel connected to others? What do expansion and growth feel like in your body?

Do you ever feel or have you ever felt a deep longing in your soul to make a change? What was the feeling like in your body?

Do it Right

Can you imagine speaking and acting so correctly that you never have to go back and apologize or make a new agreement?

What happens in your body when you realize you spoke too hastily and now have to make amends?

What happens when you check in with your body in order to support authentic choices in the moment?

Truth is Fluid

Truth can show up boldly, hurtfully, courageously, or gently. We use the compassion of nonviolence to keep truthfulness from being a personal weapon.

Have you ever used the truth (your truth) as a weapon? How did that feel in your body? In your mind? In your heart?

To be a bold person of truth is to constantly look for what we are not seeing and to expose ourselves to different views than the ones we hold sacred. Make a list of books you can read, podcasts to listen to, movies to watch, places you can go, or people you can talk with to explore alternate viewpoints. Note how you feel while learning about another viewpoint. Do you stay receptive, or do you get tense?

The Weight & Power of Truth

What are
we so afraid of?
What might our lives
look like if we were willing to
contact truthfulness in every moment?

Are you afraid to live in truthfulness? What part of you is afraid? What is your body's response to this question?

Note some ideas and beliefs that once served you, but now might be outdated. You may unknowingly be holding on to things that you no longer need. Honor these beliefs because, like a vehicle, they brought you to your current place on your journey. What does it feel like in your body when you honor them and then let them go?

Asteya
Nonstealing

We don't need what we don't need.

अस्तेय

Nonstealing

Asteya, or nonstealing, calls us to live with integrity and reciprocity. If we are living in fears and lies, our dissatisfaction with ourselves and our lives leads us to look outward, with a tendency to steal what is not rightfully ours. We steal from others, we steal from the earth, we steal from the future, and we steal from ourselves. We steal from our own opportunity to grow ourselves into the person who has a right to have the life they want.

It is easy to forget that life is a gift. Often life is challenging, difficult, lonely, and sad, but still, life is a gift. To feel the ground below our feet, to smell the air fresh from a gentle rain, to feel the warm sun on our skin, these are a few pleasures life is constantly presenting us with.

When we forget this, we easily fall prey to messages of entitlement. We somehow think we deserve to "have" and to "get." We go after things and forget to ask if we really need them. We get things and forget to say thank you. We talk about ourselves and forget to listen to others. We forget the pleasure inherent in the simple act of being in right relationship with all that co-exists with us. We end up stealing from ourselves, others, and life itself.

To live fully and faithfully, we need enough nutritious food to eat, water to drink, and air to breathe. We need a shelter that pleases us and protects us. We need the resources necessary to flourish. But we don't need what we don't need.

Life is an exchange. We receive and we give. Reciprocity is at the core of nonstealing. And gratitude is at the core of reciprocity.

Asteya: The Practice

Bring your body into cat-cow to feel the sensations of reciprocity. This can be done on hands and knees on the floor, or in a seated position. Inhale and exhale smoothly as you move between cat and cow. Can you find the balance between each shape and each breath? What does this movement of giving and receiving feel like? What can your body teach you about nonstealing? Stay here as long as you wish. Take time to reflect, journal, or be in silence with this experience. Or you may let your body move you into further exploration.

When you feel complete, intentionally choose your next activity. Whatever it is, do your best to maintain the feeling of nonstealing in your body and to consciously return to it throughout the day.

Scan the QR code below to join Deborah on YouTube for this guided practice.

The Body's Wisdom

Life is an exchange.
We receive
and we give.

What can embodying cat-cow teach you about nonstealing?

What does your body have to say? You may choose to draw pictures, write with colored pencils, or use your non-dominant hand to access your inner knowing.

Stealing from Others

When we compare ourselves to others,
we either find ourselves lacking,
which makes us feel cheated,
or we find ourselves superior,
which leaves us feeling arrogant.

When and how do you compare yourself to others? What does this feel like in your body-mind?

When and how do you steal from others through time, attention, “one-upmanship,” power, confidence, and not being able to celebrate others’ successes? Notice what is happening in you that prompts this stealing.

Now practice being a “forklift” so that everyone you come into contact with feels uplifted because they were in your presence. What needs to be happening inside you in order to be a forklift for others?

Stealing from the Earth

We are visitors to this land, to our bodies, to our minds. To fully appreciate this reality is to accept that nothing on this physical plane does or can belong to us.

Practice living as a visitor to this world, rather than an owner. List what is available to you to use and enjoy without needing to own or control (parks, libraries, concerts, sunsets). What things does your body enjoy that have nothing to do with ownership?

The ownership of things is steeped deep in our language and culture and makes it hard for us to appreciate the extent to which nothing really is ours. Watch your language of ownership this week: "my belief," "her job," "our society," etc. Let your body feel its natural place in the world. Notice the difference between "owning" and "being part of."

Stealing from the Future

Our focus seems to be on what we don't have, or what we might not have in the future, rather than on the abundance right before us.

Practice pausing on purpose, taking in what is right in front of you, and giving thanks for what you already have. What is it like to take pause? Do you feel a physical change when you pause?

How would your actions and decisions differ if you followed the wisdom to "make all decisions as if they mattered seven generations into the future"? How would you live in reciprocity with the earth and awareness of the future?

Stealing from Ourselves

We need to take time
to rest
and to reflect
and to contemplate.

In all the ways that we impose an outside image of ourselves onto ourselves, we are stealing from the unfolding of our own uniqueness. All demands and expectations that we place on ourselves steal from our own enthusiasm. All self-sabotage, lack of belief in ourselves, low self-esteem, judgments, criticisms, and demands for perfection are forms of self-abuse in which we destroy the very essence of our vitality. When we live in the past or in the future, or when we rush from one event to the next, we are stealing from ourselves. And all the ways we put up fences, whether real or imagined, around our physical belongings or around our mental idealisms, we put up barriers that steal from the full expansion of our own lives.

In what ways do you steal from your own body? How does your body let you know you are stealing from it?

Shifting our Focus

Asteya asks us to shift our focus from the other to ourselves. It asks us to get excited about the possibilities for our own life.

What are the ways you put aside your own interests? What are your reasons for ignoring your own growth potential? Does your body react when you ignore its message? In what ways?

When we attend to our own growth and learning in the area of our interests, we are engaged in the joy and challenge of building ourselves. From the fullness of our own talent and skill, we automatically serve the world rather than steal from it. What are your interests? What would you like to learn? What would challenge you and also make you joyful? What is possible for you right now? What happens in your body when you think about or engage in these things?

Building our Competence

Preparing ourselves to hold what we want is an exciting, full-time job. It moves us away from any victim stories into full responsibility for our lives. We become capable of stewarding what we ask for.

What are some of the stories you tell yourself about why you can't have or can't do the things you want? Are these stories in conflict with your body's messages?

Ask yourself, "Am I available to what I want?" Think about your dreams and goals and make a list of things to do/study/try that would increase your knowledge and competency and bring you closer to your dream/goal, thus building your *adikara*. (The Sanskrit word *adikara* means the right to know or the right to have.)

BRAHMACHARYA
Nonexcess

When gratitude and wonder
sit in the heart
there is no room for excess.

ब्रह्मचर्य

Nonexcess

Brahmacharya literally means “walking with God” and invites us into an awareness of the sacredness of all of life. This guideline is a call to leave greed and excess behind and walk in this world with wonder and awe, attending to each moment as holy.

We are living beings in need of nourishment. We need nourishment to feed the physical, mental, emotional, and spiritual levels of our being, and we receive that energy from food, movement, rest, relationships, work, and prayer.

Yet when we spend too much of the day exercising, eating, sitting, working, or on social media, we invite dullness to be our companion. Too much in the form of an extended stomach, excessive clutter, or a demanding schedule prevents life from being lived well. These things shroud our lives in a lethargic misery. We are unavailable to joy, clarity, kindness, and feelings of fulfillment.

Finding balance and moderation in all activities of life is key to accessing the inherent vitality and luster of living fully. It is also an art form to be honed. Our bodies can help us discern that place where we have had enough. If we learn to listen to our bodies, they warn us when we are about to overdo something and move into the realm of dullness.

Brahmacharya: The Practice

Come into seated boat pose of any variation. If you are sitting in a chair, raise both legs so they are extended in front of you, lifting off the floor. Whatever variation you choose, boat pose is not easy to maintain. As you need, rest, and then if you are able, come into the pose again or simply sit and experience the surge of energy at the center of your being.

What we are noticing in this pose is our core. This is the place that often feels empty, so we fill it with too much of something that feels good in the moment, but soon leaves us unsatisfied. This pose can help us discern when we are receiving energy from what we are doing, or when we are becoming dull.

Practicing this pose strengthens our core. We begin to feel the vital strength inside of us to pursue what we are really hungry for and when we are hungry for it. We gain discipline and clarity. Our willpower increases.

As dullness becomes less a part of our experience, we refuse to settle for anything less than wonder and joy. We begin to savor and stop devouring. We walk in the sacredness of what is.

Stay here as long as you wish. Take time to reflect, journal, or be in silence with this experience. Or you may let your body move you into further exploration.

When you feel complete, intentionally choose your next activity. Whatever it is, do your best to maintain the feeling of nonexcess in your body and to consciously return to it throughout the day.

Scan the QR code on the right to join Deborah on YouTube for this guided practice.

The Body's Wisdom

Finding balance and moderation in all activities of life is key to accessing the vitality of living fully.

What can embodying boat pose teach you about nonexcess?

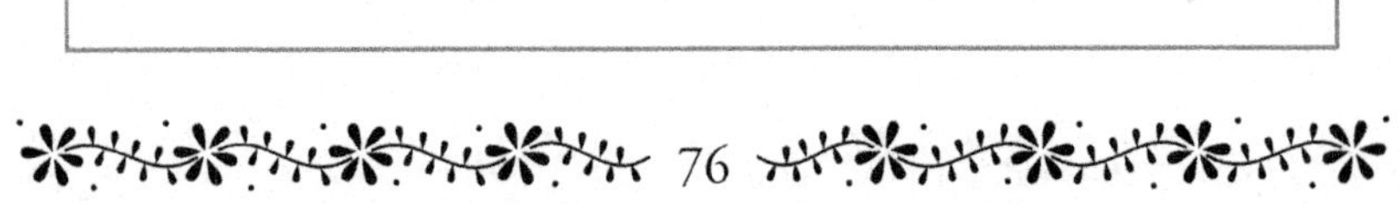

What does your body have to say? You may choose to draw pictures, write with colored pencils, or use your non-dominant hand to access your inner knowing.

Taming our Overindulgence

Whether we find ourselves overdoing food, work, exercise, or sleep, excess is often a result of forgetting the sacredness of life.

What are some of the ways you overdo it? Is it food, work, alcohol, drama, entertainment? How does your body feel when you do too much of something?

Create a do-able timeframe to practice living in nonexcess (a day, a week, etc.). Eat, work, and sleep to the point of increased energy, but before the lethargy of excess sets in. Ponder the words of Gensei, a Japanese Buddhist monk, who said, "The point in life is to know what's enough." For this timeframe, practice pleasure without excess. What do you notice in your mind and body while attempting this practice?

Celibacy

Brahmacharya reminds us to enter each day and each action with a sense of holiness rather than indulgence.

What does celibacy, or abstinence, mean to you? Do you consider it a holy path? Might there be (or have there been) times when this practice would be beneficial to your body?

Examine your beliefs, values, habits, and actions around sexuality and sexual activity. Notice what your culture, the media, your faith community, and your family have to say about this topic. Then notice if you act on outside authority, or your body's wisdom.

Vitality

Brahmacharya reminds us that we aren't embodied in this form to feel dead but to feel alive. We aren't embodied to snuff out our vitality and passion through excess but to bring it to full expression.

Do you snuff out your own vitality and passion? Why? What is so powerful about the story your mind is telling you that it overrides your body's needs? What would happen if you listened to your body instead of your mind?

Brahmacharya invites us to be willing to walk around "turned on" to the wonders of life itself. Howard Thurman understood the importance of our passion to the world when he said, "Don't ask yourself what the world needs. Ask yourself what makes you come alive. And then go do it. Because what the world needs is people who have come alive." What makes you come alive? What does aliveness feel like in your mind? In your body? In your soul?

Wonder

Seeing with the eyes of holiness shifts how we act as well as how we see. When gratitude and wonder sit in the heart, there is no need for excess.

When we see with the eyes of mystery, every task becomes an opportunity to wonder and be amazed. Mending the split between what we see as important or not, and who we see as important or not, puts us on the path to cherishing all people and all tasks. Ask yourself, "What can I do to see the divine in all things?" And, "Does my body feel differently when I see in this way?"

When the sense of wonder leaves us, when everything becomes dull and ordinary, it is often because we have kept too fast a pace for too long. We have become out of balance. It is time to rest. When rested, nothing is dull and ordinary; everything glows with mystery. What are your favorite ways to rest? What are some ways you can bring yourself back into balance in this moment?

Walking with God

Can you honor all as sacred?
Can you honor yourself as sacred?

Contemplate your own divinity. Do you treat your body as sacred? Are you willing to be sacred? Write down three practices that connect you to your passion and your sacredness. In what way is your body part of these three practices?

Where do you see God and where don't you? Notice the beliefs or judgments that limit your ability to see God and experience God in all things. Then practice letting everything be a relationship with the Divine. See the sacred in the ordinary and God in each person you encounter. Ponder the words of Yogi Bhajan, "If you can't see God in all, you can't see God at all." See God in all.

APARIGRAHA
Nonpossessiveness

A bird cannot hold its perch and fly;
neither can we grasp anything
and be free.

अपरिग्रह

Nonpossessive

Aparigraha, or nonpossessiveness, can also be interpreted as nonattachment, nongreed, nonclinging, nongrasping, and noncoveting; we can simply think of it as being able to "let go."

The word possession conjures up scenes from a horror movie where someone has been taken over by a spirit; no longer their own. This is not a pleasant thought, and yet when we try to possess something or someone, isn't this what we do? We try to control them. We try to make them do what we want.

Nonpossessiveness speaks to the relationship we have with our possessions, whether they be objects, experiences, or people. Do we appreciate them? Are we grateful for them? Or do we expect things of them and make demands on them?

"Please me." "Make me happy." "Make me feel good." These are the subtle, and not so subtle messages of possessiveness. Our refusal to share, our jealousy over another's independence, our fear of losing what we have, and our need to control and dominate are signs that indicate a violation of this restraint.

One of the purposes of life is to enjoy people, experiences, and objects. There is freedom and delight in the exchange. The problem comes when we begin expecting, even demanding, these pleasurable experiences to always make us feel good. This is not their job. This job belongs to us.

Aparigraha: The Practice

What can our bodies teach us about having joy and delight in another while at the same time feeling complete in ourselves? Come into any variation of triangle pose to explore this question. Experience the sensations of steadiness and completeness evoked by this pose. Feel your core radiating out through both legs and arms and the aliveness that fills your being. Be aware that you are complete in yourself.

As you are ready, gently take your triangle to the other side. Find the steadiness and completeness on this side. Experience your core radiating out and filling your limbs with aliveness. Think of a person, an object, or an experience that has brought you pleasure. Pay attention to the sensations that arise in your body with this thought. When you feel balanced return to a standing position. Be aware that freedom and fullness in a relation happen with the fullness and delight we have in ourselves.

Stay here as long as you wish. Take time to reflect, journal, or be in silence with this experience. Or you may let your body move you into further exploration. When you feel complete, choose your next activity intentionally. Whatever it is, do your best to maintain the feeling of nonpossessiveness in your body and to consciously return to it throughout the day.

Scan the QR code on the right to join Deborah on YouTube for this guided practice.

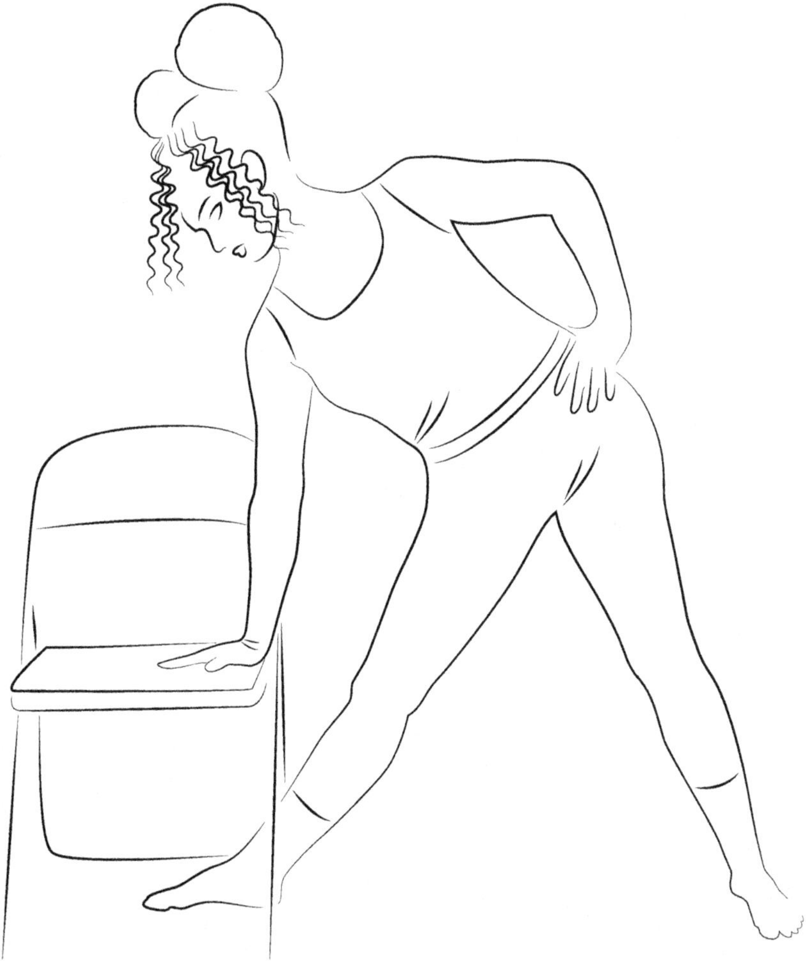

The Body's Wisdom

Can you find steadiness and completeness within yourself?

What can embodying triangle pose teach you about nonpossessiveness?

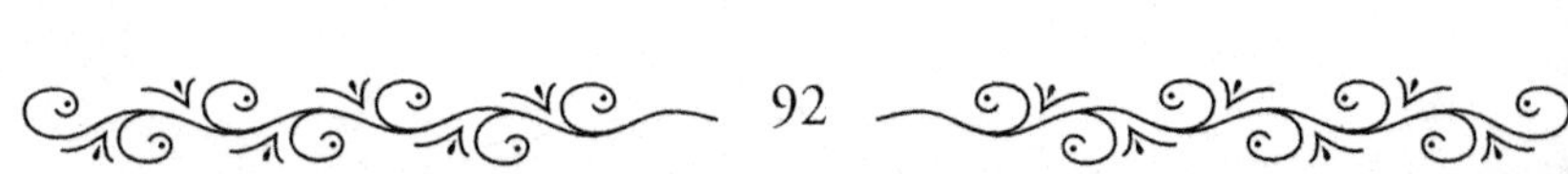

What does your body have to say? You may choose to draw pictures, write with colored pencils, or use your non-dominant hand to access your inner knowing.

The Breath

Like the breath when it is held too long, the things that nourish us can become toxic.

Pay attention to your breath. Can you let the simple act of inhaling and exhaling teach you about the fullness of breathing in life without the need to hold on to it? Journal your observations and experience.

When do you hold your breath? What purpose does holding your breath serve?

Next time you catch yourself holding your breath, see if you can breathe through the experience instead. What happens?

Letting Go

Our expectations keep us captive and often disgruntled, and yet we choose our attachments rather than our freedom.

What expectations do you place on yourself, your friends, your kids, your spouse, your parents, your government? What would letting go of your expectations feel like? Make up an experiment or think of a situation where you feel ok to let go of an expectation. What happens? Does anything change in your body?

Look at the physical things you have surrounded yourself with. Do these things make you feel free and light or do they have a hold on you and make you feel heavy?

Anything we cling to creates a maintenance problem for us (what you cling to, clings to you). Experience the difference between enjoyment and attachment. Can you feel a difference in your body? In what ways?

Over-Packing

How many suitcases full of expectations, tasks, plans, resentments, and unforgiven moments are we toting around every day?

What if we woke up every morning and took nothing with us? What if that was the whole point? What if we unpacked our way to God? Unpacked our way to freedom? Unpacked our way to being? What does unpacking look like for you? What does it feel like in your body?

What would opening yourself to vulnerability look like? Who can you trust with your true self? Make a list of true things about yourself that are usually hidden under your plans and expectations. What is your body's response as you make this list?

Nonattachment & Trust

Nonattachment frees us up to be immersed in appreciation of life and one another. It asks us to let go of the clinging to the thing, not the enjoyment of the thing itself.

Krishna Das says we have developed a strong "holding on" muscle in the mind, but the "letting go" muscle is undeveloped. He suggests we get our mind in shape by using this muscle more often, practicing with little things so we are prepared when the bigger things come along. Notice when you cling to experiences, emotions, thoughts, habits, and beliefs. Then give your "letting go" muscle some exercise and begin to let go. What are some little things you can let go of? What does your body feel like when you do?

The fewer attachments we carry with us, the more we are free to enjoy and engage and live every moment before us to the fullest. The more breath we let go of, the more room there is in our body for the fullness of the next inhalation. The more we generously share and give away, the more expansive and light we become. The journey of life is towards freedom. A bird cannot hold its perch and fly. Neither can we grasp anything and be free. What can you do to help yourself trust your journey toward freedom? What does trust feel like in your body?

Saucha
Purify

Purify your relationship with the moment.

Purity

Saucha invites us to purify our bodies, our thoughts, our words, and our relationship with the moment.

Often there is a discrepancy between what we say we want and what our calendar and checkbook tell us. Secondary pleasures and desires can easily begin to direct our daily choices, leaving us feeling fragmented and scattered. Whether it be our minds, our hearts, or our homes, we find ourselves wondering where all the clutter came from.

When something is unalloyed, it is not mixed with things that lessen its value. Gold comes to mind as one of the most obvious examples. Gold, in its close to pure state, is highly valuable. As it is mixed with metals of lesser quality and in greater quantity, its value lessens. It is the same for us.

For our lives to line up in a congruent manner, we first ask ourselves what is important to us? What has real value in our lives? And then we begin the slow and steady purging of our allurement with the things that contaminate that alignment.

Purity: The Practice

You can explore this sense of being unalloyed by bringing your body into any variation of a simple, comfortable twist. As you gently twist your body around your spine, wring out any snags that pull you out of alignment. In the same way you would squeeze excess water from a dishrag, wring your spine of the things that lessen your life.

When you feel complete on this side, return to a neutral position. As you are ready, begin to explore the twist on the other side, wringing out the things, physical, emotional, and mental, that keep you from being aligned with your higher self.

When you feel complete on this side, return to a neutral position. Feel the alignment of your spine and the spaciousness that has been created. What is your body teaching you about being pure and unalloyed with what is most valuable to you?

Stay here as long as you wish. Take time to reflect, journal, or be in silence with this experience. Or you may let your body move you into further exploration.

When you feel complete, choose your next activity intentionally. Whatever it is, do your best to maintain the feeling of this guideline in your body and to consciously return to this feeling throughout the day.

Scan the QR code on the right to join Deborah on YouTube for this guided practice.

The Body's Wisdom

Purification works on our insides and changes our very essence.

What can embodying a twist teach you about purity?

What does your body have to say? You may choose to draw pictures, write with colored pencils, or use your non-dominant hand to access your inner knowing.

Cleansing Process

Taking steps to cleanse and purify ourselves will look different for each of us.

Notice or start a list noting where/when/why your body feels heavy or sluggish and also, where/when/why your body feels light or energetic.

Do something to purify yourself through diet, exercise, breath, lifestyle, and/or changes to your environment. How does this affect your being?

What is the relationship between the external process of cleansing and the internal process of purifying? How do you feel it in your body?

Purifying the Mind

Saucha calls us to the inward journey of purification, not the external appearance of cleanliness.

Begin to purify your thoughts and speech. Identify where your mind and thoughts feel stale, negative, or toxic. What is your go-to stance / go-to complaint(s)?

Use friends, ritual, forgiveness, journaling, etc. to release toxic, stale, negative thoughts and speech. Make a list of things you are grateful for and replace the toxins with love and gratitude.

Purity in the Moment

Saucha has a relational quality that asks us not only to seek purity in ourselves, but to seek purity with each moment by allowing it to be as it is.

Can you be purely with yourself? No fixing, no should's, no insulting yourself, no expectations. In the words of Anthony de Mello, leave yourself alone. Journal the experience and what gets evoked for you. What happens in your body?

We are asked to be with life, with others, with things, with the day, with work, with the weather, as they are in the moment, not as we wish they were or think they should be or expect them to be. We fail this guideline in any of our attempts to change, judge, criticize, alter, control, manipulate, pretend, be disappointed, or check out. Where do you find yourself imposing your wishes and your will on others and on your life?

In what ways can you sit with the moment as it is rather than try to change it? Does something shift in your body?

Gathering our Scattered Pieces

Because we have not taken the time to "catch up" with ourselves, we are living on the leftovers of where we have been or the preparations of where we are going.

Purity asks that all of us be in one place at one time. And that means that our head, heart and body are unified, our thoughts, actions, and speech are congruent, and we are in the present moment.

In what ways do you feel scattered? What does scattered feel like in your body?

Where do you feel unified in mind, body, spirit and purpose? When does your heart feel filled with compassion? What do you want to do about these noticings?

Santosha
Contentment

The moment is complete as it is.

Contentment

Santosha invites us into contentment by taking refuge in a calm center, opening our hearts in gratitude for what we have, and practicing the paradox of "not seeking."

Contentment is such a fleeting thing. We enjoy it for periods of time, and then, just like that, it slips through our fingers, reminding us once again that it can't be held. Like a constant roller coaster ride, we are tossed high and low between gratification and disgruntlement. Our happiness depends on the success of our hopes, expectations, and preferences being met in the moment. What a tiring way to live.

The key to understanding contentment is to admit how much we demand that life fulfills our desires in each and every moment…so much so that we are willing to give away our own life force, emotional stability, and happiness. But life was not made to satisfy our every whim, and we were not made to become rigid, weak, and intolerant slaves to our partiality.

We are passengers on a journey called life. We can plug in a route for the scenic ride, but ultimately the route is not ours to determine. What we do have control over is what kind of passengers we will be. Will we enjoy the ups and downs of the journey, challenging ourselves to stop complaining and keep breathing? Can we maintain gratitude for the gift of the ride itself, no matter how bumpy?

Contentment: The Practice

Gently bring yourself on your back and come into happy baby pose. If this pose is uncomfortable, bring yourself into a variation of bear pose. Let your arms and legs dangle in the air, rocking and moving as you wish.

Give yourself permission to be playful and childlike. Can you find the body memory of being a baby in your crib and playing with your feet? Being in endless wonder about your toes, even putting them in your mouth?

What sensations and feelings are moving through you? What is the experience of being lost in the contentment and exploration of your own being? What is it like to need nothing in the moment except to be here?

Stay here as long as you wish. Take time to reflect, journal, or be in silence with this experience. Or you may let your body move you into further exploration.

When you feel complete, choose your next activity intentionally. Whatever it is, do your best to maintain the feeling of contentment in your body and to consciously return to this feeling throughout the day.

Scan the QR code on the right to join Deborah on YouTube for this guided practice.

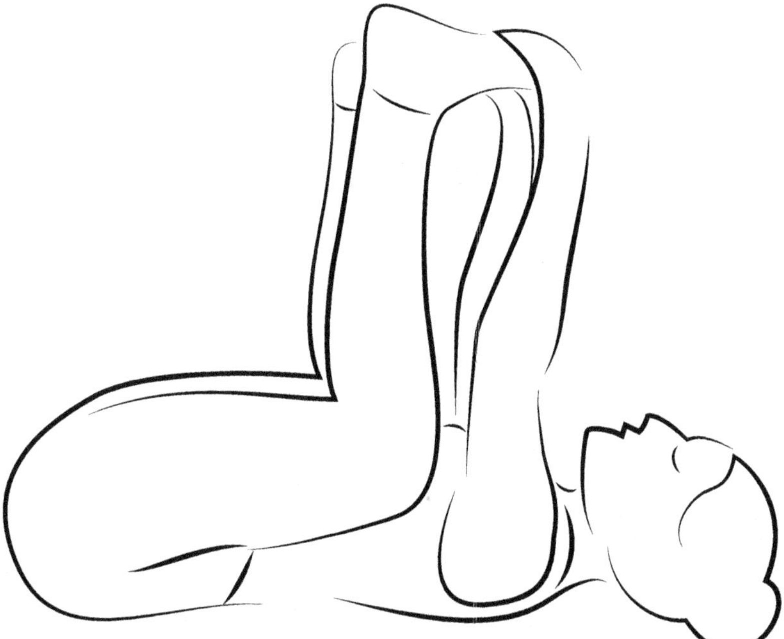

The Body's Wisdom

Santosha invites contentment by taking refuge in a calm center.

What can embodying happy baby pose teach you about contentment?

What does your body have to say? You may choose to draw pictures, write with colored pencils, or use your non-dominant hand to access your inner knowing.

Looking Outward

Looking outward for fulfillment will always disappoint us and keep contentment one step out of reach.

When we expect the world to meet our needs, we turn outside of ourselves to find sustenance and completion. We expect our partners to fulfill us, our jobs to meet our needs, and success to solve all of our problems. What expectations do you hold for others' behavior toward you? What do you expect from your job? Do you think life owes you something?

Americans are often "getting ready." We can't wait to grow up; we can't wait to take a vacation; we can't wait to retire. We let our contentment be managed by uncontrollable variables. As long as we think satisfaction comes from an external source, we can never be content. Notice when you find yourself getting ready for the next thing or looking for contentment from something outside of yourself. In what ways do you look outside yourself to find contentment? How does looking outside yourself feel in your body?

Pleasure & Avoidance

Seeking and avoiding are expensive uses of our energy.

We spend vast amounts of our lives moving towards what we like, whether the object is food, clothes, colors, music, self image, conversation, hobbies, friends, activities, or beliefs. Likewise, we move away from what we don't like. We think we are free but in truth we are ruled by our preferences. Notice how much energy you expend moving towards what you enjoy and avoiding what you dislike. Notice any physical gripping sensations in your body. Journal what you notice.

If you really want to shine a light on your attachments, you might do this experiment: try spending a few days doing what you don't like and not doing what you do like and see how attached you are to your preferences. What do you notice in your mind's stories, your attitude, your excuses, your body, etc.

The yogis tell us that things are neutral. It is the personal labeling we put on these things that makes them appealing or repulsive to us. What can you re-label "neutral" in your mind that was previously something you sought or avoided?

Emotional Ups & Downs

When we give the power of our emotional state to someone or something outside of ourselves we have made ourselves helpless.

Carlos Castaneda writes, "Our self-importance requires that we spend most of our lives offended by someone." In what ways do you spiral into emotional and energetic loss over feeling offended? How does this spiral feel in your body?

Can you take responsibility for all your emotional disturbances? Can you trace every annoyance and upset back to yourself? Do you choose to stay in the disturbance or to return to the calm center of contentment (or to be content with your disturbance)? What is it like to take responsibility for all of your emotional states? How can your body help you take responsibility?

Gratitude

Practicing gratitude protects us from
our own pettiness and smallness
and keeps us centered in
the joy and abundance
of our own life.

When stimulation pulls at us and disturbance beckons us, it is the gratitude uttered from our lips that keeps us strongly rooted in contentment. But it is not easy in this culture to stay contented. So how do we get there and how do we stay there? How do we live with a feeling of abundance? How can your body help? Jot some ideas.

When gratitude slips out of our hearts, we are left vulnerable to the rumblings of discontentment. To counteract this, you might play the "thank you game." What, with some kind of honesty, can you say thank you to in life? What happens in your body when you say thank you?

The Paradox of Not Seeking

Discontentment is the illusion that there can be something else in the moment. There isn't and there can't be. The moment is complete.

Santosha, or contentment, is the true understanding that there is nothing more that can or does exist than this very moment. Practice bringing your mind to this moment, to this body, to this breath, to this experience, time after time. What do you notice?

It is easy to be content when we feel great and things are going our way and we like ourselves. But what about when chaos and interruptions abound, or we are sick or in pain, or feeling bored or depressed? What then? Can you practice being content with discontentment? What does this feel like in your body? Journal what you notice.

Tapas
Self-Discipline

Discipline is something we prioritize, we carve space for, and we attend to.

तपस्

Self-Discipline

Tapas is our determined effort to become someone of character and strength.

Things are happening at a fast pace in our modern world. We feel it, we try to keep up with it, we long to slow it down. Yet there often remains a level of inertia in us, hidden by the shadows of our busy days. There is a hesitation to be burned by the fire of transformation. The pleasures of escape are inviting and easily accessible, and there is always tomorrow to get serious about discipline.

This guideline stands as a reminder that the only way to get from where we are to where we want to be is through the fire of discipline. Like a raw egg submits to the frying pan and emerges with entirely different properties or a log submits to a fire and becomes more like the fire than the log it once was, self-discipline invites us to submit to an uncomfortable process.

The discomfort is leaving our warm bed to go to our mat and cushion. The discomfort is in drinking turmeric tea instead of a sugary coffee drink. The discomfort is speaking out against prejudice and violence. The discomfort is in looking at the selfishness, greed, and hatred that sit in our own hearts. And the power is in being willing to submit to this discomfort day after day after day.

Self-Discipline: The Practice

Gently bring yourself into any variation of warrior I pose and begin to experience the strength this posture invites. Claim the stamina and courage that allow you to meet the challenges of the day with grace and dignity.

As you feel complete on this side, reverse sides, continuing to find steadiness in the transition. Find the strength to stay when quitting would be easier. Honor your determination to give yourself to something greater.

When you feel balanced on both sides, return to standing pose. Breathe deeply, and take for your own the indomitable spirit of the warrior. How does this feel in your body?

Remember that discipline is something you prioritize, you carve space for, and you attend to. You claim it as important and deserving of your attention, and you choose it at the expense of other things.

Stay here as long as you wish. Take time to reflect, journal, or be in silence with this experience. Or you may let your body move you into further exploration.

When you feel complete, intentionally choose your next activity. Whatever it is, do your best to maintain the feeling of discipline in your body and to consciously return to it throughout the day.

Scan the QR code below to join Deborah on YouTube for this guided practice.

The Body's Wisdom

Self-discipline is the determination to give yourself to something greater.

What can embodying warrior pose teach you about self-discipline?

What does your body have to say? You may choose to draw pictures, write with colored pencils, or use your non-dominant hand to access your inner knowing.

Catharsis

It is the times of hopeless desperation that shape and mold us into someone of depth.

Tapas can take us to the place where all of our resources are used up, where there is nothing left but weakness, where all of our so-called "props" have been taken away. It is in this barren place, where we have exhausted all that we have and all that we are, that new strength is shaped and character is born if we choose to fearlessly open ourselves to the experience. It is perhaps the greatest gift life could offer us. What are some examples in your life where all your reserves were used up? How did you feel?

Charlene Westerman speaks truthfully to the danger and the possibility of catharsis when she states that during these times we have two choices: to break down or to break open.

Remember the cathartic times in your life and how you were shaped by them. Notice the times you may have "checked out" from the pain, and others where you were fearless in the fire and held on for the blessing. Did you notice a different feeling in your body when you "held on" instead of "checking out"?

Daily Practice

What are we practicing for? When is the last time you even asked yourself this question?

We can't prevent times of catharsis in our lives or know their shape or outcome, but we can prepare ourselves for them through our daily practice, through building our ability to stay in unpleasantness, and through the small, daily choices we make. What practices do you have that help you build your strength of character? Is there a daily practice you would like to do?

In yoga, having a daily disciplined practice is referred to as *Sadhana* (spiritual practice) and is much like doing a small controlled burn on ourselves. This week choose a practice of nourishing eating, meditating, contemplating, or something else that impacts the quality of your essence. Can you put yourself in the heat with enthusiasm?

Staying Power

In those times when we don't know how to get through the next minute of what seems unknown and overwhelming to us, can we hold on until we are somehow blessed by our struggle?

So often we don't even know what has us in its grip; it seems dark and overpowering. In those times, can we hold on, gripping it back, and not letting go until we are somehow blessed by it? Can we grow our ability to stay in the fire and let ourselves be burned until we are blessed by the very thing that is causing us the pain and suffering?

Practice staying one minute more when unpleasantness arises. Can you stand the heat of unpleasantness? Can you let the heat begin to burn away your judgments, opinions, and expectations? How do you feel when you stay one minute more?

Crisis & Choice

Tapas is the willingness to be both burned and blessed.

Each moment is an opportunity to make a clear choice of right action. Quite often the choices that prepare us for the fire are options that vote against immediate satisfaction and pleasure. Name some times you have made choices for future growth or future benefit. When were some times you took the "easy road"? Did your body respond differently to these two choices?

During crisis, if we can choose to strengthen our inner depth rather than medicate and run, we will find ourselves in a land of new possibility. The promise of a crisis is that it will pick us up and deposit us on the other side of something. How can your body support you to trust this process?

Can you pay attention to your daily choices? Are you making choices that are indulgent, or making choices that build your strength and character? Listen to your inner voice and make choices that prepare you for the heat of life.

Svadhyaya
Self-Study

What is left if all the descriptions of ourselves disappear?

स्वाध्याय

Self-Study

Svadhyaya, or self-study, is knowing our true identity as Divine, which creates a pathway to freedom.

Throughout our lives, nouns and adjectives get placed on us. These words help describe our own uniqueness, and that can be beneficial. But when these words become the limits of our identity, we find ourselves trapped into thinking that this is all there is to us. We become a noun rather than a process of becoming. We become who others tell us we are.

Wisdom teachers inform us that there is more to us. We are not just one possible form that the mystery creates, but we are actually the mystery itself. That we don't fully grasp this concept is in part because we are holding on tightly to the nouns and adjectives that limit us.

What is left if all the descriptions of ourselves disappear? This is the bigger question that self-study asks. Who am I? Why am I here? Where did I come from? The mystic Francis of Assisi is reported to spend long evenings alone in a cave, repeating the question, "Who am I God, and who are you?" "Who am I God, and who are you?"

We can begin to ask ourselves these bigger questions. We can watch our projections, trace our reactions back to a belief, and courageously look at life as it is. We can ask ourselves, "Who am I, really?" The process of knowing ourselves creates a pathway to freedom.

Self-Study: The Practice

Bring yourself into down dog, modifying the posture as needed. Gaze back on yourself and ask, "Who am I when all the adjectives and nouns are taken away?" "Who am I, really?"

Stay in this pose or come into a comfortable seated position, continuing to repeat these questions. "Who am I when all the adjectives and nouns are taken away?" "Who am I, really?"

Be in the wonder of the yet unknown mystery of yourself.

Stay here as long as you wish. Take time to reflect, journal, or be in silence with this experience. Or you may let your body move you into further exploration.

When you feel complete, intentionally choose your next activity. Whatever it is, do your best to maintain the feeling of self-study in your body and to consciously return to it throughout the day.

Scan the QR code on the right to join Deborah on YouTube for this guided practice.

The Body's Wisdom

We suffer
because we forget
who we are.

What can embodying down-dog
teach you about self-study?

What does your body have to say? You may choose to draw pictures, write with colored pencils, or use your non-dominant hand to access your inner knowing.

Projections

We cannot love or hate something about another person or the world unless it is already inside of us first.

Do this experiment now: without thinking, quickly write down the first five things that come to your mind that describe the world as you see it. Now look at what you have written. Every comment that you have used to describe the world will tell you more about yourself than about the world. You have just written clues into how you structure your beliefs, yourself, and your life. Every comment you make about the world, about another person, about an event, about life, is a projection of yourself and a clue to your interior landscape. What are you telling yourself?
What does your body feel?

Others reflect back to us what we see in ourselves. What are you projecting onto others that is really about parts of yourself that you love, don't love, can't see, or can't yet accept?

The world reflects what you believe. You can experiment with this truth by changing the story about what you see. Does the world look different when you do this? Has the world changed, or have you?

Tracing it Back

Tracing any disharmony back to ourselves will help us unpack a box in which we have wrapped ourselves.

Usually we don't notice our beliefs or conditioning unless there is some kind of disharmony present. Discover this by tracing all ripples of disharmony back to yourself. Notice what personal belief system caused the disharmony.
Is your belief true? Are you experiencing reality or a box?

Ninety-nine percent of what bothers you is about you. Ninety-nine percent of what bothers others has nothing to do with you. Do you turn the above statements around, blaming others for your own problems and taking responsibility for others' problems? Practice taking responsibility for yourself and letting others be responsible for themselves. What do you notice? What shifts in your body?

Afraid to Look?

We need our eyes and hearts wide open to look at every ripple of disharmony that we experience.

If we hide reality from ourselves, how can our hearts grow? If we close our eyes, our very lives rest on a false foundation. We can't be afraid to look. The guideline of Svadhyaya invites us to see all; not to shut the unpleasant parts of ourselves away, but to carry them with kindness and compassion, knowing that God lives here too. What are you afraid to look at?

The reality of what sits inside us can be great, beautiful, and terrible. And whatever we pretend isn't there will unconsciously rule us. But we can choose to feed the beauty and grow ourselves into someone more compassionate and kind to both ourselves and to others. We must be willing to look at the selfishness, fear, greed, and anger that lie in us, but feed the greatness. What is the "greatness" in you?

Role of Ego

When Ego acts as the boss, we believe we are separate, and we make our belief system the model of reality. When this happens, we run on old habits and we consent to being less than we are.

The ego is a function of the mind that organizes itself into "I." The ego is not a bad thing; without the ego, we wouldn't exist. It gives us the experience of separateness. Name ways you think and act as if you were the center of the universe.

When the ego forgets that its function is to organize the self and begins to believe itself to be the boss, we get stuck in the "I" of being separate, and we make our belief system the model of reality. Our belief system is not wrong or right, but it is constraining; when we identify with these constraints, we run on old habits and we consent to being less than we are. In what ways are you being constrained by outdated identities and beliefs? Where do you feel this in your body?

The Power of the Witness

The witness is our ability to watch ourselves act and respond. It is this ability to watch that begins to bring healing to our lives.

In western culture, we tend to analyze, fix, and control just about everything. In Eastern thought, the "power of the witness" is a way to distance ourselves from ourselves, and begin to see our made up realities. And paradoxically, it is how our belief system begins to lose its hold on us. In what ways do you analyze, fix, and control? How do these things feel in your body?

Meditation is an important aspect of self-study; it is a place where we grow the witness, recognize our belief systems, and begin to shift our identity from our bodies and minds to the Godself within. Grow the power of your witness by watching all your actions and thoughts as if you were watching a movie. What do you notice about yourself? Does your body feel different when you are in a witness stance? In what way?

As we shift our attention to the Divine within, the boxes of belief systems begin to fall away, and we become free. We rest in our true Self. What does this feel like for you?

Ishvara Pranidhana
Surrender

You are held, guided, and loved through every moment of your life.

ईश्वर प्रणिधान

Surrender

This guideline invites us to surrender our egos, open our hearts, and accept the higher purpose of our being.

Ishvara Pranidhana, or surrender, presupposes that there is a divine force at work in our lives. Whether we call it God, grace, providence, or life, this force is greater than we are and cares deeply about us. Surrender invites us to be active participants in our life, totally present and fluid with each moment, while appreciating the magnitude and mystery of what we are participating in. Ultimately this guideline invites us to surrender our egos, open our hearts, and accept the higher purpose of our being.

You may have experienced the beauty of surrender when you were caught up in something you love to do. Suddenly time disappeared and you disappeared with it. Your actions, your thoughts, and the activity you were engaged in, lined up and became one entity of harmony and perfection. This is the rhythm of surrender.

The yogis tell us that we can live this way all the time, unless we are getting in our own way.

Oh, how we love to get our way. Full of demands and expectations, we work to manipulate and control the moment. Like toddlers throwing a tantrum from their highchair, we complain loudly when life doesn't happen on our terms.

The truth is, we can attempt to control our lives with plans and expectations. Or we can surrender to them. We can meet our lives with ease, dancing with each moment as it is, trusting that we are being cared for.

Surrender: The Practice

Lie down and make yourself comfortable. Feel the tension leave your body as you give yourself to the floor. The yoga posture called savasana, or corpse pose, is a posture for practicing surrender. Putting ourselves on our backs, with our arms and legs at a forty-five degree angle from the body, signifies the death of the activity we have just participated in. It is also a practice for the ultimate surrender of our own death.

In savasana, there is nothing for us to do. We are asked to just lie there, releasing any tension in our bodies, letting go of effort, and trusting that the breath will breathe us and the body will renew itself. (If this sounds easy, it's not.) Savasana is one of the most important practices we can do, for it is here that we begin to learn the meaning of letting go of all the ways we physically and mentally fight with life.

As you lie here, reflect on the mystery of your life and the goodness that sits in the very fabric of the universe. Reflect on the brilliance of the stars, the vastness of the universe, the smell of pine trees, the exquisiteness of flowers, the taste of strawberries.

In all of this, you matter. You are an intricate and unique song that this mystery is singing. And you are held, guided, and loved through every moment of your life. Whatever this mystery is that cares for the universe, intimately cares for you.

As you lie here, be attentive to what is presenting itself without trying to change it. Let go of expectations and preconceived ideas. Just breathe, and let this moment be what it is.

Stay here as long as you wish. Take time to reflect, journal, or be in silence with this experience. Or you may let your body move you into further exploration. When you feel complete, intentionally choose your next activity, doing your best to maintain the feeling of being intimately loved and cared for. Return to this feeling often throughout the day.

Scan the QR code on the right to join Deborah on YouTube for this guided practice.

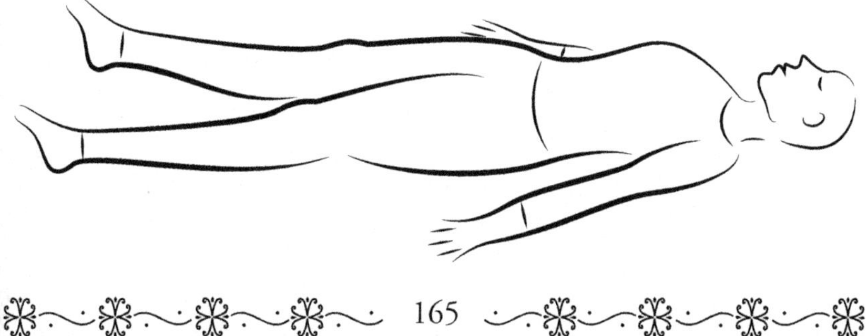

The Body's Wisdom

Let go of expectations and preconceived ideas. Just breathe, and let this moment be what it is.

What can embodying savasana teach you about surrender?

What does your body have to say? You may choose to draw pictures, write with colored pencils, or use your non-dominant hand to access your inner knowing.

Releasing

As we learn to stop fighting life, we can begin to act skillfully.

How do you feel when you lie still on your mat? Can you let go of tension and your to-do lists? What is your mind telling you as you lie here? What is your body telling you?

Control makes us rigid and tight and narrows our perspective. Getting rid of our armor opens a world of possibility and makes us lighter and more comfortable for the journey. We can monitor our moment to moment surrender to life by watching the inner sensations of contraction and expansion. Contraction is a feeling of constriction, a pulling in. Expansion is an opening, a creating of space and wonder. When we find ourselves in contraction, we are fighting life or fearful of life. When we find ourselves in expansion, we are in the flow of surrender.

When do you find yourself in contraction? What does it feel like in your body? In your mind?

When do you find yourself in expansion? What does it feel like in your body? In your mind?

Engaging

Surrender asks us to be strong enough to engage each moment with integrity, while being soft enough to flow with the current of life.

Like white water rafting, surrender is learning to skillfully ride with what the moment gives us, all the while enjoying the process, whether we glide through safely or tip over and get wet. In what ways do you skillfully navigate your life?

In what ways do you resist what life is giving you, waging war on the moment by demanding that it gives you what you want, just the way you like it?

Ignoring or resisting what is in front of you is like trying to make the current do what we want it to. That attitude is disastrous on a raft, and it is disastrous in life. When we need life to be a certain way, we get restricted and tight, rather than open to the current of life. But each time we ride the rapids, we become a more skillful paddler. Practice welcoming each moment and growing yourself into the opportunity of what is being offered and asked of you. What bodily sensations do you notice when you are welcoming?

Accepting

Our task is to let go
and receive each moment
with an open heart.

For this practice, I invite you to watch your attitude and responses to the moment. Are you fearful, trusting, fighting, joyful, judging, accepting, annoyed? Notice if there is a pattern to your reactions. What do you notice in your body?

Do you notice any tension that arises in your body when you need the moment to be "your way"? Consciously choose to relax your body and shift your attitude to curiosity. Notice what happens. How do you feel? What is your mind telling you? Can you, as Buddha inspires, "Cease to cherish your beliefs"?

Devotion

Ishvara Pranidhana is the surrender of the ego to a higher purpose. As the ego stops fighting to be number one, life begins to nourish and feed us in amazing ways.

Surrender is ultimately a stance of devotion that takes place in the heart and permeates all of our attitudes and actions. In its deepest sense, Ishvara Pranidhana is the surrender of the ego to a higher purpose. As the ego surrenders, the heart expands. As the ego stops working so hard to get its own way, life begins to take on an ease and rhythm. As the ego stops fighting to be number one, life begins to nourish and feed us in amazing ways. What does it feel like when you let go of answering to the ego?

As we grow ourselves into the fullness of what this guideline has to teach us, we begin to understand the magnanimity of what guides, protects, nourishes, and cares for us. Surrender is knowing ourselves to be a part of this Divine Oneness and then giving ourselves over to this greater whole.

Create a statement that includes yourself as part of everything (for example, "I am one with All") and then tell it to yourself many times a day. Believe in something that is greater than you are and let your actions, your mind, your body, and your heart line up with that greatness. What is your statement?

How does it feel in your heart, mind, and body to be connected to all things?

Contrast & Shadow Work

A Shortcut to Insight & Alignment

As we grow in awareness of the subtle and not so subtle ways we transgress these ethical principles, it becomes clear that we need the body on board to lay down new neuropathways that put us in right relationship with life.

After writing the yamas and niyamas, I found I needed a shortcut—something that would provide quick insight into my behavior both when I was aligned and misaligned with each of these ethical principles. I named this shortcut, "triggers & practices" (pgs. 180-191).

After my experience with the taxi driver (refer to p. 8-9), triggers & practices became a way to not only notice my behavior, but to feel it in my body. The value of this grew as I noticed it was my body that signaled a transgression before I noticed my behavior.

I quickly discovered that when I was misaligned, my muscles were tense and my breath was shallow. In contrast, when I was in alignment with the guidelines, there was a sense of ease. I always felt a softening, a release, and an easy breath.

We deal with emotions that include anger, disappointment, neediness, impatience, frustration, sadness, restlessness, grief, fear, and anxiety to name a few. These emotions beg to be acknowledged and gently led to a place of resolution.

When we pretend we aren't angry, for instance, or try to suppress our anger, we paradoxically promote anger. If we are pretending to be nice when we are seething inside, everyone loses. In any way that we "make" ourselves conform to our conceptual ideas of who we should be, we lose the chance to hear the body's voice.

The intent to "soften into" rather than to deny or suppress what we are feeling is critical. To acknowledge these emotions as they arise and give them space to find a harmonious resting place is not only powerful work, it is the path to transformation.

Throughout this book, we have practiced becoming familiar with the body's experience of being aligned with each guideline. To practice contrast, or shadow work, is to become familiar with what it feels like in the body when we are misaligned with these guidelines. Shadow work, as I am using it here, is the awareness of our anger, irritation, etc. as it arises, acknowledging it, and softening into it.

Shadow work sheds light on the habitual tension we carry, a tension we barely notice because it feels normal. In this work, we are bringing awareness to our conscious mind of how unpleasant this tension is. We are also bringing awareness to the ways tension in our bodies offers insight into the subtle ways we are out of alignment.

Although I find this exploration of contrasts in part unpleasant, I also find it informative and enlightening. My body is becoming insistent on being in a harmonious state. It longs to soften into the experience, whether it is a pleasant or an unpleasant one. I'm sure my body has always longed to be in ease, it's just that I have been so occupied with the story my mind is telling me, I have failed to notice.

When we are without excess tension, the body is fluid and grounded. We have access to the wholeness and authenticity of our being. This is where the voice of wisdom can be heard. Tension shuts this down and denies us access to clarity.

When we relax, the body becomes saturated with spaciousness, and things begin to harmonize within us and around us. We can't make ourselves relax, we can only soften into the muscles, thoughts, and emotions. From this place, we are trustworthy participants in the cosmos, acting harmoniously and appropriately.

As we practice contrast and shadow work, it becomes apparent that we can't conceptually master anything. The body is a clear definer of the subtle and not so subtle ways we offend harmony. The body has much to say. And when we listen, we are able to respond with more clarity and compassion.

How to Practice

On the following pages you will find the trigger & practice for each guideline with space below it to write your observations and sensations after your exploration. If you find your experience different from mine, make the words and experience relevant to you.

When you are ready to practice contrasts, take one guideline at a time. Go slow. Begin with nonviolence. Reflect on the times you have been irritated, angry, impatient, unkind, or just plain mean. Allow yourself to feel how this expresses itself in your body. What do you notice? Where do you notice it? What is happening with your breath? This is not a pleasant experience, and your body will soon tell you that you are violating the undergirding foundation of first, do no harm.

Now soften into any tension. Notice the shift. What changes? Explore this practice with each of the yamas & niyamas. Remember, we are not in any way denying the unpleasant emotion, we are inviting the body to soften into it.

Also remember, we are not trying to fix ourselves or change ourselves. The practice here is to focus our awareness on the body and away from the "cause" of the trigger. This is a powerful shift of awareness. It is here that we gain freedom from identifying with our habitual response. As we soften into the tension, the softening itself begins to ground and purify us.

Triggers & Practices Overview

Yamas

Nonviolence

Trigger: agitation, impatience, irritation
Practice: friendliness

Truthfulness

Trigger: judgment
Practice: beginner's mind

Nonstealing

Trigger: greed
Practice: generosity

Nonexcess

Trigger: overwhelm
Practice: periodic fasting from technology, food, speech, purchases

Nonpossessiveness

Trigger: neediness
Practice: letting go

Triggers & Practices Overview

Niyamas

Purity

Trigger: image
Practice: simplicity

Contentment

Trigger: comparison, expectation
Practice: gratitude

Self-Discipline

Trigger: entitlement, escape
Practice: responsibility

Self-Study

Trigger: blame
Practice: curiosity

Surrender

Trigger: resistance
Practice: trust

Nonviolence

My trigger: agitation, impatience, irritation
Your trigger:

My practice: friendliness
Your practice:

What happens in your body when you are triggered? Is there tension? Where do you feel it? Does it have a texture or a color? What is happening to your breath? Journal or draw a picture of your experience.

Now soften and breathe into the tension. Does something change? Is there movement? Let the process happen without imposing an agenda on it. What do you notice?

Truthfulness

My trigger: judgment
Your trigger:

My practice: beginner's mind
Your practice:

What happens in your body when you are triggered? Is there tension? Where do you feel it? Does it have a texture or a color? What is happening to your breath? Journal or draw a picture of your experience.

Now soften and breathe into the tension. Does something change? Is there movement? Let the process happen without imposing an agenda on it. What do you notice?

Nonstealing

My trigger: greed
Your trigger:

My practice: generosity
Your practice:

What happens in your body when you are triggered? Is there tension? Where do you feel it? Does it have a texture or a color? What is happening to your breath? Journal or draw a picture of your experience.

Now soften and breathe into the tension. Does something change? Is there movement? Let the process happen without imposing an agenda on it. What do you notice?

Nonexcess

My trigger: overwhelm
Your trigger:

My practice: periodic fasting from tech, food, speech, purchases
Your practice:

What happens in your body when you are triggered? Is there tension? Where do you feel it? Does it have a texture or a color? What is happening to your breath? Journal or draw a picture of your experience.

Now soften and breathe into the tension. Does something change? Is there movement? Let the process happen without imposing an agenda on it. What do you notice?

Nonpossessiveness

My trigger: neediness
Your trigger:

My practice: letting go
Your practice:

What happens in your body when you are triggered? Is there tension? Where do you feel it? Does it have a texture or a color? What is happening to your breath? Journal or draw a picture of your experience.

Now soften and breathe into the tension. Does something change? Is there movement? Let the process happen without imposing an agenda on it. What do you notice?

Purity

My trigger: image
Your trigger:

My practice: simplicity
Your practice:

What happens in your body when you are triggered? Is there tension? Where do you feel it? Does it have a texture or a color? What is happening to your breath? Journal or draw a picture of your experience.

Now soften and breathe into the tension. Does something change? Is there movement? Let the process happen without imposing an agenda on it. What do you notice?

Contentment

My trigger: comparison, expectation
Your trigger:

My practice: gratitude
Your practice:

What happens in your body when you are triggered? Is there tension? Where do you feel it? Does it have a texture or a color? What is happening to your breath? Journal or draw a picture of your experience.

Now soften and breathe into the tension. Does something change? Is there movement? Let the process happen without imposing an agenda on it. What do you notice?

Self-Discipline

My trigger: entitlement, escape
Your trigger:

My practice: responsibility
Your practice:

What happens in your body when you are triggered? Is there tension? Where do you feel it? Does it have a texture or a color? What is happening to your breath? Journal or draw a picture of your experience.

Now soften and breathe into the tension. Does something change? Is there movement? Let the process happen without imposing an agenda on it. What do you notice?

Self-Study

My trigger: blame
Your trigger:

My practice: curiosity
Your practice:

What happens in your body when you are triggered? Is there tension? Where do you feel it? Does it have a texture or a color? What is happening to your breath? Journal or draw a picture of your experience.

Now soften and breathe into the tension. Does something change? Is there movement? Let the process happen without imposing an agenda on it. What do you notice?

Surrender

My trigger: resistance
Your trigger:

My practice: trust
Your practice:

What happens in your body when you are triggered? Is there tension? Where do you feel it? Does it have a texture or a color? What is happening to your breath? Journal or draw a picture of your experience.

Now soften and breathe into the tension. Does something change? Is there movement? Let the process happen without imposing an agenda on it. What do you notice?

Conclusion

When the yamas and niyamas
are rooted down through our body
and into the earth,
we become an embodied presence,
potent and alive.

As we explore ethics through postures, it is valuable to remember that postures did not originally come from a book; they came from curiosity and experimentation. The first yogis asked themselves, "Hey, I wonder what it is like to be a tree? Or a cobra? Or a cow?" We are asking similar questions, "Hey, I wonder what it is like to be nonviolent? Or truthful? Or content?"

So be curious, explore, experiment, and see what can be learned, felt, and known about the yamas and niyamas through the wisdom of your body. Take a few minutes in the morning, in whatever way you choose, to ground your body, mind, and day in these principles of right relationship.

To behave with integrity is a soothing balm in a world inundated with violence. To live in right relationship with others is healing medicine. The body can help us understand what integrity and right relationship are; the body can support our sense of intimacy with the world. The body can teach us to fall in love with our humanness.

When the yamas and niyamas are rooted down through our body and into the earth, we become an embodied presence, potent and alive.

Author Bio

Deborah Adele holds master's degrees in both Liberal Studies and Theology & Religious Studies. She carries yoga certifications in Kundalini yoga, Hatha yoga, Yoga Therapy, and Meditation. She is also trained in Gestalt Theory and Somatic Education. From 1999 to 2012, Deborah brought her combined knowledge of business and her in-depth knowledge of yoga philosophy to build Yoga North, a center that continues to flourish.

In 2009 she published *The Yamas & Niyamas: Exploring Yoga's Ethical Practice*, which has become an international best-seller an a modern classic. It is a go-to book for any serious yogi and for anyone seeking deeper understanding of self.

Deborah's writing and teaching leave participants with a dynami combination of hope, inspiration, and practical knowledge.

Visit Deborah at www.DeborahAdele.com.

Books by Deborah Adele

The Yamas & Niyamas: Exploring Yoga's Ethical Practice

The Kleshas: Exploring the Elusiveness of Happiness

The Yamas & Niyamas Embodied: A Companion Journal

Available at your favorite bookstore and on amazon.com. (Scan QR code on right to see Deborah's books on Amazon.)

Videos by Deborah Adele

The Yamas & Niyamas: Explanation and Overview

The Kleshas: Explanation and Overview

The Yamas & Niyamas Embodied: Guided Meditations

To behave with integrity is
a soothing balm in a world
inundated with violence.

To live in right relationship
with others
is healing medicine.

The body can help us understand
what integrity and
right relationship are.

The body can support
our sense of intimacy
with the world.

The body can teach us
to fall in love
with our humanness.

~ Deborah Adele

Printed in Great Britain
by Amazon

61334834R00111